DOGS WITH JOBS

Sled Dogs

Faith Woodland

MEDIA ENHANCED BOOKS AV2 BY WEIGL ADDED VALUE • AUDIO VISUAL

www.av2books.com

Published by AV^2 by Weigl
350 5th Avenue, 59th Floor
New York, NY 10118
Website: www.av2books.com

Library of Congress Cataloging-in-Publication Data
Names: Woodland, Faith, author.
Title: Sled dogs / Faith Woodland.
Description: New York, NY : AV2 by Weigl, [2020] | Series: Dogs with jobs | Audience: Grade 4 to 6. | Includes index.
Identifiers: LCCN 2018053544 (print) | LCCN 2018054177 (ebook) | ISBN 9781489699008 (Multi User Ebook) | ISBN 9781489699015 (Single User Ebook) | ISBN 9781489698988 (hardcover : alk. paper) | ISBN 9781489698995 (softcover : alk. paper)
Subjects: LCSH: Sled dogs--Juvenile literature.
Classification: LCC SF428.7 (ebook) | LCC SF428.7 .W66 2020 (print) | DDC 636.73--dc23
LC record available at https://lccn.loc.gov/2018053544

Printed in Guangzhou, China
1 2 3 4 5 6 7 8 9 0 23 22 21 20 19

012019
103118

Editor: Katie Gillespie Art Director: Terry Paulhus

Weigl acknowledges Getty Images, Alamy, and iStock as its primary image suppliers for this title. Every reasonable effort has been made to trace ownership and to obtain permission to reprint copyright material. The publishers would be pleased to have any errors or omissions brought to their attention so that they may be corrected in subsequent printings.

CONTENTS

Capable Canines

Have you ever gone down a hill on a sled and wished you had help pulling the sled back up to the top? Perhaps you needed a sled dog.

Sled dogs are specially trained dogs that are **harnessed** to sleds of various sizes. They are used to pull all sorts of things across icy or snowy **terrain**.

Sleds may be pulled by one or two dogs, or by a large team. Teams of sled dogs are arranged in pairs.

A person stands on the back of the sled as a driver or "musher." This person gives the dogs directions. The musher also works a brake with his or her foot.

Sled Dog History

Dogs have pulled sleds for more than 1,000 years. North American **Aboriginal** people used dog sleds as their main mode of **transportation**. Up to three dogs were harnessed to a sled to carry food, firewood, and furs.

French Canadian trappers used dog sleds to follow their trap lines and transport animal skins. They used the French word *marche* to tell their dogs to run. This command was misunderstood as "mush," which became the term for sledding.

In the 1700s, Russian explorers began arranging dogs in pairs or single file with a trained **lead dog** at the front. Demand for sled dogs increased during the Alaskan Gold Rush of the late 1800s. **Miners** needed to bring food, bedding, tools, and equipment into the mountains as they went in search of gold. Early sleds were made of wood, with smooth runners to glide swiftly across the snow.

Sled Dogs Today

With the invention of snowmobiles and helicopters, sled dogs are no longer depended upon for transportation in the North. However, dog sledding remains popular as a recreational activity. Many people go on dog sled rides for fun as part of an outdoor winter camping adventure or northern tour.

Dog sled racing is also a popular sport. Every winter, teams of dogs and drivers compete in long races across the northern wilderness. Races such as the Iditarod and Yukon Quest cover approximately 1,000 miles (1,600 kilometers) and take about two weeks to complete.

FACTS UNLEASHED

In 2010, the first Jamaican sled dog team competed in the Iditarod with driver "Mushin' Mon" Newton Marshall.

WARNING
AVISO

Sled Dog Life

Sled dogs live and work together as a group. Each dog has his or her own shelter or dog house. These houses are arranged in rows, and may be made of plastic barrels or wooden boxes.

Shelters help protect the dogs from rain and snow, although sled dogs do not really mind the cold. Houses can be lined with straw for comfort. The dogs are chained to posts outside their houses, which gives them room to walk around, but does not let them get away, otherwise they might be off and running!

Sled dogs are fed multiple times a day. They eat meat or fish, and combinations of fats, oils, and dry dog food. Racing dogs are given vitamin supplements as well. During races, they eat up to 10,000 **calories** of food a day, which is five times more than the average person eats.

Training

Sled dogs begin training at a very young age. Owners touch the puppies often to get them used to being handled. They use a collar and let the puppies drag a leash.

At 10 weeks old, a sled dog puppy is introduced to a harness, which it wears around its body. By four months of age, a puppy will pull a light object, such as a log, across dirt or grass. Puppies in training are given lots of encouragement and treats.

Sled dogs also learn to wear waterproof booties. These help protect their feet from the rugged landscape. During the Iditarod, each dog must have eight extra pairs of booties on the sled.

The driver teaches the puppy special commands for driving. The word "gee" means right and "haw" means left. The command "leave it" is used when the puppy must ignore an object. The trainer uses the word "easy" to slow the puppy down.

Sled dogs must learn how to work as a team. They are all harnessed to a main **gangline** or **towline**, usually in pairs. Certain dogs are trained to be lead dogs. They run at the front of the pack. The lead dogs are followed by swing dogs, team dogs, and wheel dogs. There may be 12 to 16 dogs in a full Iditarod racing team.

While in training, sled dogs work very hard. They run for five to six hours a day, five to six days per week. During the off-season, they go on short distance runs.

FACTS UNLEASHED

Sled dogs that compete in races train all year. They face challenges such as winter storms, freezing temperatures, and running across rough, icy snow.

The Great Race of Mercy

In 1925, an outbreak of a deadly disease called diphtheria occurred in Nome, Alaska. There was no way for planes or ships to take medicine to the people in danger. Instead, multiple teams of dogs relayed the special serum across miles (km) of frozen land from Anchorage to Nome.

This event became known as The Great Race of Mercy. It took six days for 20 mushers and 150 dogs to cover 674 miles (1,000 km). The teams traveled over icy terrain, through blizzards and darkness.

Balto, a dog on loan to Gunnar Kaasen by Leonhard Seppala, was the lead dog on the last leg of the journey that brought the medicine to the desperate villagers. In 1995, Universal Pictures made a movie entitled *Balto*, about the heroic sled dog. There is also a statue of Balto in New York City's Central Park.

Another heroic sled dog named Togo, also owned by Seppala, led the longest, most difficult stretch of the race. Togo ran a round trip of 365 miles (587 km). A statue of Togo was erected in New York City's Seward Park.

All of the dogs and mushers involved in The Great Race of Mercy were heroes. They accomplished a difficult goal. Their story shows how people and animals can work together.

Sled Dog Safety

When visiting a dog sled team or taking part in a tour, it is important to follow any instructions given by the handlers. Sled dogs are very strong and energetic. They can take off running at any opportunity.

Sled dogs must be handled firmly, following the correct procedure. You should never walk between harnessed dogs, as you could become tangled in the lines and pulled by the dogs. Always ask an owner for permission to approach a dog or a team. While most dogs are friendly and love attention, you need to respect their need for space as well.

What Makes a Good Sled Dog?

Today, most sled dogs are a mix of different breeds. Many sled dogs are Alaskan huskies. Over time, sled dogs have been bred with Siberian huskies and greyhounds to increase their speed.

Sled dogs must have tough feet, a thick coat of fur, healthy appetites, and an urge to run. They need to be able to endure the cold climate, and travel on snow and ice. Sled dogs cannot be lazy. The best sled dogs are the ones that think "somewhere else is better" and just want to go running to find that place.

FACTS UNLEASHED

Each year, the Leonhard Seppala Humanitarian Award is given by race veterinarians to the musher who takes the best care of his or her dog team during the Iditarod race.

Quiz

1 What is the special name for a dog sled driver?

2 What did early sled dogs transport?

3 What event in the late 1800s increased the demand for sled dogs?

4 How many calories must a racing dog consume each day during racing season?

5 Which two inventions decreased the need for sled dogs as transportation in the North?

6 What are the dogs at the front of a team called?

7 What do the terms "gee" and "haw" mean?

8 Where is the statue of Balto located?

9 In what state did the 1925 outbreak of diphtheria take place?

10 How long was the Great Race of Mercy?

ANSWERS
1 Musher 2 Food, furs, and firewood 3 The Alaskan Gold Rush 4 10,000 5 Helicopters and snowmobiles 6 Lead dogs 7 Right and left 8 Central Park in New York City 9 Alaska 10 674 miles (1,000 km)

Key Words

Aboriginal: original inhabitant

calories: units of energy

gangline: the main rope or line to which sled dogs are harnessed

harnessed: fastened to a sled by a set of straps

lead dog: the dog at the front of the team

miners: people who work underground in a mine to obtain minerals, such as gold, coal, or diamonds

terrain: a stretch of land

towline: a rope or cable used for pulling a sled

transportation: the act of transporting or moving something

Index

Log on to www.av2books.com

AV² by Weigl brings you media enhanced books that support active learning. Go to www.av2books.com, and enter the special code found on page 2 of this book. You will gain access to enriched and enhanced content that supplements and complements this book. Content includes video, audio, weblinks, quizzes, a slide show, and activities.

AV² Online Navigation

Audio
Listen to sections of the book read aloud

Book Pages
AV² pages directly correspond to pages in the book.

Video
Watch informative video clips.

Embedded Weblinks
Gain additional information for research.

Key Words
Study vocabulary, and complete a matching word activity.

Try This!
Complete activities and hands-on experiments.

Quizzes
Test your knowledge.

Slide Show
View images and captions, and prepare a presentation.

AV² was built to bridge the gap between print and digital. We encourage you to tell us what you like and what you want to see in the future.

Sign up to be an AV² Ambassador at www.av2books.com/ambassador.

Due to the dynamic nature of the Internet, some of the URLs and activities provided as part of AV² by Weigl may have changed or ceased to exist. AV² by Weigl accepts no responsibility for any such changes. All media enhanced books are regularly monitored to update addresses and sites in a timely manner. Contact AV² by Weigl at 1-866-649-3445 or av2books@weigl.com with any questions, comments, or feedback.